THE ATTACK
ON
PEARL HARBOR
IN UNITED STATES HISTORY

THE ATTACK ON PEARL HARBOR

IN UNITED STATES HISTORY

IN
UNITED STATES
HISTORY

★ NATHAN ANTHONY ★
AND ROBERT GARDNER

Enslow Publishers, Inc.
40 Industrial Road
Box 398
Berkeley Heights, NJ 07922
USA

http://www.enslow.com

Originally published as *The Bombing of Pearl Harbor in American History* in 2001.

Library of Congress Cataloging-in-Publication Data

Anthony, Nathan.
    [Bombing of Pearl Harbor in American history]
    The attack on Pearl Harbor in United States history / Nathan Anthony and
Robert Gardner.
      pages cm. — (In United States history)
      Original edition published under title: The bombing of Pearl Harbor in
American history. Berkeley Heights, NJ : Enslow, 2001.
      Includes bibliographical references and index.
      ISBN 978-0-7660-5448-6
      1. Pearl Harbor (Hawaii), Attack on, 1941—Juvenile literature. I. Gardner,
Robert, 1929– II. Title.
      D767.92.A72 2014
      940.54'26693—dc23

                          2013044460

Future Editions:
Paperback ISBN: 978-0-7660-5450-9
EPUB ISBN: 978-0-7660-5451-6
Single-User PDF ISBN: 978-0-7660-5597-1
Multi-User PDF ISBN: 978-0-7660-6057-9

Printed in the United States of America
072014 HF Group, North Manchester, IN
10 9 8 7 6 5 4 3 2

To Our Readers: We have done our best to make sure all Internet addresses in this book were active and appropriate when we went to press. However, the author and the publisher have no control over and assume no liability for the material available on those Internet sites or on other Web sites they may link to. Any comments can be sent by e-mail to comments@enslow.com or to the address on the back cover.

Illustration Credits: Enslow Publishers, Inc., p. 18; National Archives and Record Administration (NARA), pp. 3, 39; Stasys Eidiejus/Hemera/©Thinkstock, p. 11.

Cover Illustrations: The *USS Arizona* (BB-39) burning after the Japanese attack on Pearl Harbor, 7 December 1941, National Archives and Records Administration (NARA).

☆ CONTENTS ☆

☆ INTRODUCTION ☆

Early in the morning of December 7, 1941, all was quiet at Hawaii's Pearl Harbor Naval Base. War was on the horizon for the United States, but the fleet was not on alert. Instead, sailors slept peacefully or ate a relaxed breakfast on their ships. No one thought of the threat posed by faraway Germany and the war in Europe. No one even thought much about the signs that Japan—a little more than three thousand miles away—was preparing for war.

In 1941, war was on the minds of people around the world. In Europe, Germany and Italy were fighting the "Allied" countries, which included Great Britain and the Soviet Union. Germany had already invaded and defeated Poland, France, Yugoslavia, and most of Europe. Many people in America worried that soon Germany would defeat England and the Soviet Union and then attack the United States. Winston Churchill, the leader of Great Britain, wanted the United States to help fight against Germany.

Still, most Americans did not want to fight in a war in Europe. Many politicians and celebrities were isolationists—those who did not want the United States to fight in a foreign war. Other

Americans had heard stories of Germany's persecution and killing of European Jews and other minorities, and wanted to help Great Britain and the Soviet Union defeat Germany. These people argued that the leader of Germany, Adolf Hitler, must be stopped before it was too late.

While Americans debated joining the war in Europe, they also feared the possibility of war with Japan in the Pacific Ocean and Asia. Japan was an ally of Germany. Military leaders in Japan wanted to expand their empire in the Pacific, but the United States was in the way. The United States had military bases on many islands in the Pacific and could easily attack Japan at any time. Earlier, Japan had invaded China and northern Indochina (part of which is now Laos and Vietnam). Japanese soldiers in Nanking and Shanghai, China, had been especially ruthless. Accounts of Japanese actions in Shanghai caused widespread horror in the United States. When Japan later invaded southern Indochina, the United States responded by refusing to supply Japan with oil. Japan needed American oil to power its military. This angered the Japanese and relations between the two countries worsened. If Japan could not buy oil from America, they would take it from somewhere else.

The situation had reached the point where many American leaders, both at Pearl Harbor and in Washington, expected war. Only ten days earlier, Admiral Husband Kimmel, Commander in Chief of the Pacific Fleet, had received a strong message from the Department of the Navy in Washington, which said, "This dispatch is to be considered a war warning. . . . An aggressive move by Japan is expected within the next few days." Still, few people believed that the Japanese would attack Pearl Harbor—it was too well defended.[1]

Before World War II, most of the United States Navy fleet was stationed at Pearl Harbor. The naval base was so big that the entire United States Navy could dock, get fuel and supplies, and be repaired at one time. Pearl's shape—large, with a narrow entrance—made it one of the best harbors in the Pacific. Forts on either side of the entrance, along with coral reefs, were a barrier to any attack. In addition to the tens of thousands of naval officers and midshipmen stationed at Pearl Harbor, more than twenty-five thousand Army, Air Force, and Marine Corp soldiers were also stationed on the island of Oahu to help protect the harbor and the people of Hawaii.[2]

On December 7, 1941, the war began dramatically for the United States. The Japanese Navy successfully launched a sneak attack on the United States bases at Pearl Harbor, Hawaii. Thousands of Americans died and many more were wounded in the attack. The raid on Pearl Harbor damaged or destroyed many of the United States naval ships in the Pacific Ocean. The event forced America to enter World War II, fighting not only Japan, but also Japan's European ally, Germany. It was not until 1945 that the United States and its allies finally defeated Japan and Germany and ended World War II.

For the Japanese, the Pearl Harbor operation was highly successful. The Japanese military lost few planes in the attack and succeeded beyond their wildest expectations. With much of the American Pacific fleet destroyed or disabled, the attack cleared the way for more than six months of Japanese dominance in the Pacific. The Pearl Harbor attack showed the Japanese military at its best: organized, disciplined, and intelligent.

For Americans, Pearl Harbor will always be a "date which will live in infamy" as President Franklin Delano Roosevelt described it. Caught completely by surprise, Americans were embarrassed and angered by the attack. Many responded by enlisting in the armed forces to fight the Japanese and Germans, while others helped to

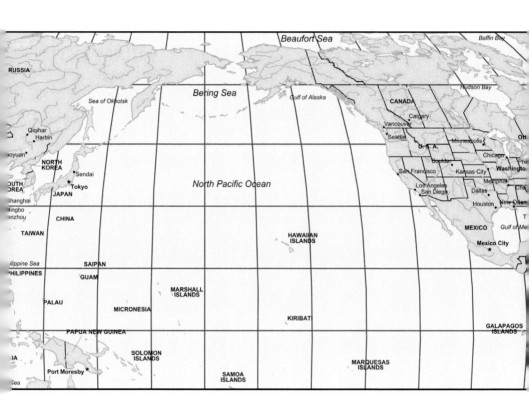

North Pacific Ocean

quickly rebuild the fleet. In just over six months, the American Navy had recovered enough to defeat the Japanese at the Battle of Midway.

It all began that morning, December 7, 1941, with an attack on Pearl Harbor.

Chapter 1

THE DAY BEFORE

Just before three o'clock in the afternoon of December 6, 1941, Takeo Yoshikawa walked out of the Japanese consulate in Honolulu, Hawaii, on the island of Oahu. He stepped into a taxi and set out for nearby Pearl Harbor to locate and count the American warships there. He had made this count many times and reported his findings to military officials in Japan. In this December report, he listed 9 battleships, 3 light cruisers, 3 submarine tenders, and 17 destroyers at anchor, and 4 light cruisers and 2 destroyers at the docks. He added that all the heavy cruisers and aircraft carriers had left Pearl Harbor. Upon completing his report Yoshikawa returned to his quarters and relaxed.[1]

Takeo Yoshikawa was a Japanese spy. In Japan, Yoshikawa had been trained as a naval officer until a stomach ailment put an end to his early ambitions. After years of studying, Yoshikawa improved his English and learned everything he could about the United States Navy. Yoshikawa came to Oahu as a diplomat in March 1941 and began reporting on the size and the strength of the United States Navy at Pearl Harbor.[2]

Yoshikawa and the Japanese military knew that Pearl Harbor was a very important military base for the United States. The Hawaiian Islands are located in the center of the Pacific Ocean and ships can quickly sail from Pearl Harbor to Alaska, California, Japan, or Australia. Sometimes called the crossroads of the Pacific, Hawaii is about 2,000 nautical miles from San Francisco and 3,300 nautical miles from Japan.

That evening a dance was taking place at the Pearl Harbor Officers' Club. Admiral Husband Kimmel attended a small dinner party, which he left at 9:30 P.M. Returning to his quarters, he went to bed immediately, planning to rise early and play golf with Army General Walter Short. Short had gone to a dinner dance, which he left between 10:30 and 11:00 P.M. He and his wife and another couple drove past Pearl Harbor; home to the United States Pacific Fleet. One hundred and three vessels sat in the harbor that evening. Seeing the lights of all the ships aglow, Short commented: "Isn't that a beautiful sight? What a target they would make!"[3]

In Honolulu, the evening of December 6 was typical. Many enlisted men spent their Saturday night at the Black Cat Cafe, Bill Leader's Bar, and the Bloch Recreation Center. At the Recreation Center, the finals of a "Battle of Music" decided the best band in the Pacific Fleet. Bands from four ships competed in a contest which was won by the band from the battleship *Pennsylvania*. Ensign Everett Malcolm of the battleship *Arizona* did not start home until 2:00 A.M., having spent the evening with his fiancée. Realizing it was too late to return to the ship, he went to the home of the ship's dentist. There, he joined the dentist and several other young officers sitting on the floor arguing about history and politics.

A fighter pilot, Lieutenant Kermit Tyler, was driving to work at that hour. He had the 4-to-8 A.M. shift at the army's new information center at Fort Shafter, several miles east of Pearl Harbor. This was the nerve center of the aircraft warning service. Tyler was to begin duty at Fort Shafter for only the second time. If an air attack was detected it was Tyler's job to alert the Pearl Harbor defenses.

On his way to the fort, he turned on his car radio and listened to Hawaiian music. Three hundred miles to the north, Commander Kanjiro Ono heard the same music. On board the Japanese aircraft carrier *Akagi*, Ono was part of a large Japanese force that was quickly approaching Pearl Harbor. The Japanese fleet included four aircraft carriers with over 350 planes, 30 submarines, 5 midget submarines, and 15 other ships. Despite the size of the Japanese fleet, no one at Pearl Harbor knew they were there. The ships sailed swiftly through the rough seas, preparing for their attack.[4]

Chapter 2

WAR OR PEACE?

As in the United States, many people in Japan feared a major war between the two countries. The United States was a much larger country with many natural resources. Japan had to import oil, steel, and almost everything else it needed. A long war would be difficult for Japan to win. The only hope for Japan was for a quick war or a peace agreement.

In 1941 the Japanese government made plans for both. Under the direction of Admiral Isoroku Yamamoto the Japanese military drew up plans to attack Pearl Harbor and destroy the entire Pacific fleet of the United States Navy. At the same time, the Japanese government sent a representative to negotiate for a peace agreement with the United States.

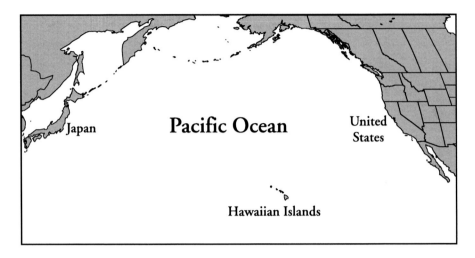

The Pacific Ocean

Japanese and American officials found it very difficult to agree on anything. They met from February to December, but ultimately agreed on nothing. The Americans insisted that Japan could not take over other Asian nations, but the Japanese disagreed.

With little confidence in the peace negotiations, Isoroku Yamamoto devised a military plan for defeating the United States. Born in 1884, Isoroku Yamamoto studied in the United States at Harvard University. He quickly rose through the Japanese Navy and became Navy Minister in 1936. Yamamoto believed that Japan could not hope to win a long war and that Japan should be in a position to defeat the United States as soon as possible after war started. When the Japanese premier asked him how he thought an attack on America would turn out, Yamamoto replied that he anticipated victory provided that the war was over within a year—"But after that I am not at all sure."[1]

Yamamoto was very determined. After seeing successful mock raids by carrier-based Japanese torpedo bombers that spring, he reportedly said to his chief of staff: "It makes you wonder whether we couldn't launch an air attack on Pearl Harbor."[2]

Yamamoto's plan was simple. The Japanese navy needed to get to Hawaii secretly and surprise the United States. Planes could take off from Japanese aircraft carriers and attack Pearl Harbor, shooting, bombing, and torpedoing American ships, airplanes, and army bases. Midget submarines could also secretly enter Pearl Harbor and attack American ships from underwater. The key to the plan was secrecy. If Americans were ready for the attack then they could fight back and destroy the Japanese force. It was a risky plan, but Yamamoto felt it was Japan's only chance to win a war.[3]

After Yamamoto convinced other Japanese military leaders that his plan was their best chance to win the war, he began to organize the task force that would sail to Hawaii. The task force included aircraft carriers, destroyers, subs, and midget submarines. The midget submarines were designed to be small enough to get into Pearl Harbor and avoid American anti-submarine nets.

Admiral Yamamoto had issued an order early in November setting "X Day" as December 8, in Japan, which would be Sunday, December 7, in Honolulu. To get into position on time, the strike force had to leave on November 25. Yamamoto chose December 7 because the American ships were normally at anchor on Sundays. It was also one of the last days before bad winter weather would threaten the operation.

Up until December 6, the Japanese high command could change its mind about attacking, and the strike force could be recalled. This would happen if the strike force was detected or the peace negotiations resumed. If the strike force was discovered on the seventh, the decision to withdraw or attack was up to the strike force's leader.

The Japanese ships had to keep complete radio silence, even in the thickest fog. Even one radio message could help the Americans discover the task force and ruin the surprise. The ships could communicate only by flashing signals.

On December 1, Japanese leaders agreed they could not accept the United States' terms for the peace negotiations. The final decision for war was made. However, they did not formally tell the Americans that they were ending the negotiations until after the attack had already begun.

The next day Yamamoto radioed a succinct message: "Climb Mount Niitaka 1208"—the code words for "Proceed With Attack" at midnight on December 8 (Japan time). A crewman on one of the ships recorded his thoughts: "An air attack on Hawaii! A dream come true!"[4]

As the strike force closed in on its target, the seas grew calmer and the fog lifted. This good fortune was countered by bad news in a message from Tokyo: there were no aircraft carriers at Pearl Harbor. This was a tremendous disappointment to Commander Minoru Genda. If the Japanese could destroy American aircraft carriers, United States forces would be unable to wage an air war across the Pacific. Genda told Commander Ono, who was in charge of communications for the strike force, that if only two carriers turned up he would not mind if all eight battleships in the harbor—the biggest prize left—were missing.[5]

Another disappointment was that none of the fleet was anchored in Lahaina Roads, on the west coast of the Hawaiian island of Maui. This area had sometimes been used as an anchorage for the fleet in the past. Lahaina was much deeper than Pearl Harbor and any ship sunk there could never be salvaged.

Ahead of the strike force, thirty Japanese submarines patrolled the Oahu area. Their mission was to sink any United States warships that might escape the air attack. Five of the submarines also carried midget subs which they planned to release near Pearl Harbor. These small subs only had two crew members. Carrying two torpedoes, the midget subs had the potential to cause significant damage to American ships.

On December 5 the strike force was 600 miles north of Oahu. The nervous Japanese pilots wrote letters or tossed restlessly in their bunks as they waited to complete their mission.[6]

Chapter 3

EARLY WARNINGS

As the Japanese fleet approached Pearl Harbor, the Americans still had a chance to discover the attack. It would not be easy. There were very few clues, but in the moments before the attack, Americans received early warnings of the Japanese operation. In the waters off of Oahu, American ships discovered Japanese submarines. After the Japanese launched their planes, a radar screen showed the approaching Japanese planes. If the Americans were to discover the Japanese attack, someone would have had to guess what the clues meant.

A Submarine Is Spotted

At about 1:00 A.M. on December 7, the Japanese submarines neared Pearl Harbor and released the midget subs. Only one of the five made it to Pearl Harbor.

In the early hours of December 7 before the attack, another Japanese midget submarine was involved in an incident. The U.S. destroyer *Ward* and two minesweepers, *Condor* and *Crossbill*, were patrolling the entrance to Pearl Harbor. Suddenly, *Condor's* officer of the deck, R. C. McCloy, saw what he thought to be a submarine periscope. *Condor* sent a report to the *Ward*, whose skipper, Lieutenant William W. Outerbridge, was awakened. Outerbridge searched for an hour. He found nothing, and at 4:35 A.M. sent his men back to their bunks. He did not report the incident. Neither did *Condor* or *Crossbill*.

Two hours later Outerbridge was awakened again by a lookout. This time there was no doubt that a small submarine was fifty yards away, and *Ward* attacked it with gunfire and depth charges—explosive devices designed to explode underwater. Depth charges were used throughout the war to destroy submarines.

This time the depth charges worked. The sub, most likely the same one that survived earlier, sank. Outerbridge quickly reported this incident to Pearl Harbor. In his message, at 6:53 A.M., he said, "We have attacked, fired upon and dropped depth charges upon submarine operating in defensive sea area."[1]

The radio officer on watch at Pearl Harbor was Lieutenant Commander Harold Kaminsky. He immediately tried to telephone his superior officers. He had trouble reaching some of them. When he finally reached an officer, the official thought the submarine reports were likely false. Another, the staff duty officer, finally reached Admiral Husband Kimmel at about 7:40 A.M. The admiral decided to wait for verification before doing anything. Despite the attack, Pearl Harbor was not put on alert.

Radar

Aboard the Japanese carriers, pilots assigned to the first wave of the attack met for a breakfast of rice and red beans. The seas were heavy as big waves rocked the Japanese ships. The air attack commander, Mitsuo Fuchida, would not have allowed his pilots to take off if it had been only an exercise. But 250 miles north of Pearl Harbor, at 6:15 A.M., the 184 planes in the first attack wave took off. One plane crashed into the ocean, but within minutes, the rest were in the air and moving toward Pearl Harbor. The 167 planes in the second wave were then brought on deck, prepared for flight, and about an hour later launched in still rougher seas. A group of fighter planes followed the bombers to provide protection.

In his plane, Fuchida heard a weather report between songs on KGMB and directed his pilots to home-in on the station. The clouds broke at 6:57 A.M., and an almost theatrical red dawn over Oahu filled Fuchida with awe. He knew nothing of the submarine sinking. Nor did he know his planes were on the Americans' radar.

Near the northern tip of Oahu, Private Joseph L. Lockard and Private George E. Elliott operated a mobile radar unit. They were to go off duty at 7:00 a.m., when the unit closed. This Sunday morning, Lockard began to shut down the radar, but Elliott asked him to hold off so he could have some practice using it. Lockard waited a bit, then looked at the screen over Elliott's shoulder. At 7:02 A.M., the two men saw a big blip approaching Oahu from the north. Lockard and Elliott believed the radar blip represented a group of at least fifty planes. Lockard telephoned Lieutenant Kermit Tyler at the Fort Shafter information center to tell him about the blip.

Radar was a new invention in 1941 and still in the experimental stage. The army was still training its operators, and most did not know how to use the equipment. Radar operators could not tell friend from foe and did not even know when their own Army or Navy flights were coming to Pearl Harbor. No one realized at the time how important radar could be for protecting Pearl Harbor from an air attack.

Tyler remembered hearing KGMB's Hawaiian music on his car radio at 3:00 A.M. as he drove to work. A friend had told him the station played music all night long when American B-17 bombers flew in from California. Recalling what his friend had said, Tyler thought the blip represented the bombers coming from California. But the B-17s, then on their way to bolster U.S. forces in the Philippines, were close, but not yet visible on the radar screen. Assuming they were indeed what Lockard and Elliott had picked up on their screen, Tyler simply said to Private Lockard, "Well, don't worry about it," and did nothing further about the matter.[2]

Lockard argued a little, then gave up and again started to shut down his equipment. Once more Elliott persuaded him to keep it going. The two men watched the blip until they lost it at 7:39 A.M. in echoes from the mountains around them. As the blip finally disappeared, the best chance to warn the Pearl Harbor fleet had been missed.[3]

The morning was unusually beautiful. Far above Opana, Commander Fuchida saw the sun come up and clouds billowing below him. He began to worry whether he and the other pilots would be able to see their target. Then, as he squinted through his binoculars, the clouds parted and he saw the great vessels in Battleship Row and all the other ships glistening in the sun. He thought, "God must be with us!"

At 7:49 A.M., ten minutes after Lockard and Elliott lost their blip, Fuchida signaled the 183 planes in the first wave to attack: *"To, To, To"*—the first syllable of *totsugekiseyo*, the Japanese word for "charge."[4]

Chapter 4

THE ATTACK

The attack on Pearl Harbor began at 7:56 A.M. on December 7, 1941. As church bells rang and many soldiers and sailors ate their breakfast, Japanese planes descended on Pearl Harbor and the nearby army bases.

Kakeuchi Takahashi, leading the dive bombers, plunged toward the Pearl Harbor Naval Air Station on Ford Island and dropped the first bomb. It hit a seaplane ramp, sending up a shower blast of water and mud.

Rear Admiral William Furlong saw the bomb falling. He was waiting for breakfast on the quarterdeck of his flagship *Oglala*, an old minelayer. Furlong thought an American pilot had dropped the bomb accidentally. Then Takahashi banked and the admiral saw the rising sun emblems on the airplane's wings. "Japanese! Man your stations!" Furlong shouted.[1]

At the same moment, Lieutenant Commander Logan Ramsey, standing at a window of the Ford Island command center, saw the bomb explode and ran to the radio room. He ordered the radio operators to broadcast on all frequencies in plain English, "Air raid, Pearl Harbor. This is NOT drill!"[2] At 7:58 A.M., this message went out to the commander of Pearl Harbor, Admiral Husband Kimmel, to Washington, and to the headquarters of the United States Asiatic Fleet in the Philippines.

In Washington, where it was 1:30 P.M., the Ford Island message was brought to Secretary of the Navy Frank Knox, who exclaimed, "My God! This can't be true, this must mean the Philippines!" Assured that it was indeed Pearl Harbor, Knox telephoned the White House, where President Roosevelt was with Harry Hopkins, his closest civilian aide. Hopkins, a former secretary of commerce, was also surprised. "Surely Japan would not attack in Honolulu," he said. But Roosevelt said he thought "it was just the kind of unexpected thing the Japanese would do."[3]

Battleship Row

The main targets for the Japanese attack were the eight battleships. *Nevada, Arizona, West Virginia, Tennessee, Oklahoma, California,* and *Maryland* were moored in "Battleship Row." *Pennsylvania* was in dry dock across the channel. The Japanese had hoped to destroy the three American aircraft carriers, but none was in Pearl Harbor that day. By good fortune one aircraft carrier, *Enterprise,* and several other ships were delayed returning to Pearl Harbor by rough weather and narrowly missed the attack.

The first wave of Japanese planes wasted little time and took advantage of the surprise. Some planes, equipped with torpedoes that could go through the water and explode when they hit a ship, approached their targets just fifty feet in the air. The planes launched their torpedoes and quickly flew away to prepare for a second run. All the battleships on Battleship Row were hit by torpedoes.

Another group of Japanese dive bombers and horizontal bombers attacked in lots of waves. Horizontal bombers dropped their bombs from high in the air, away from American anti-aircraft fire. Dive bombers flew high, but dove toward their target, dropped their bombs, and then flew away. Bombs from both kinds of planes hit battleships as well as other ships and army bases around Pearl Harbor.

Arizona

In the moments before the Japanese attacked, Marine Major Alan Shapley enjoyed a big breakfast on the battleship *Arizona*. As coach and first baseman of the ship's baseball team, he was looking forward to the fleet championship game that afternoon. Shapley had not finished his pancakes when he heard a loud bang and ran out on deck. Some sailors at *Arizona's* rail were watching planes race across the harbor, circling in figure 8's and dropping bombs. One of the sailors said admiringly: "This is the best . . . drill the Army Air Force has ever put on!"[4]

Fifteen-year-old U.S. Seaman Martin Mathews, who had lied about his age when he enlisted, was visiting with a friend on *Arizona* when they heard the first bomb explosions. The General Quarters alarm sounded, telling everybody to go to the battle stations, but Mathews did not know what to do. He normally worked at the Ford Island Naval Air Station. "I had no place to go," he remembered. "I didn't even know what General Quarters was. So

I just stayed in the back part of the ship. Pandemonium broke loose; sailors were running everywhere. It was a state of confusion."[5]

Explosions kept hitting the *Arizona*, rocking the ship, and Mathews suddenly found himself in the water. *Arizona* had been hit by a bomb that landed on one of its guns and blew up the forward magazine where shells and explosives were stored. The explosion killed nearly a thousand men and sent many more flying into the water. In minutes, *Arizona* was in flames and sinking. After swimming to a nearby buoy, Mathews recalled seeing "steel fragments in the air, fire, oil—God knows what all—pieces of timber, pieces of boat deck, canvas, and even pieces of bodies. . . . It's far too much for a boy of fifteen years old to have seen."[6]

When general quarters was sounded on the *Arizona*, Shapley went up the ladder to his post, a fire control station on the mainmast. But the ship was already on fire. Shapley ordered his men to go back down and save themselves. When the bomb hit the forward magazine, he was sent hurtling into the water, partly paralyzed by the shock and without his clothes, which were blown off by the explosion.

Earl Nightengale was also in the water. He tried to swim but could not. Following the explosion, oil leaked into the harbor and many sailors found it difficult to swim in the oily water. Shapley, who had begun to recover from the shock and was able to swim, seized Nightengale by the shirt and told him to hang onto his shoulders. The exhausted Shapley soon had to pause. Nightengale let go and told the major to go on alone but Shapley refused. Somehow mustering up the strength, he pulled Nightengale to safety.

When they finally made it ashore on Ford Island, some of their badly burned shipmates were already there, "moaning and walking around in a daze" from the shock, Shapley recalled. He wandered around himself, still naked, until someone gave him some clothing and a glass of whiskey.[7]

USS *Arizona*'s senior surviving officer, Samuel Fuqua, helped the few others who survived to leave the ship. Earl Pecotte, ordered by Fuqua to jump off, asked Fuqua if he himself was going to swim ashore. "Not until the Japs leave," was the reply. He won the Medal of Honor.[8]

On shore, Admiral Husband Kimmel was on the telephone when a sailor rushed in to tell him: "There's a message from the signal tower saying the Japanese are attacking Pearl Harbor and this is no drill!"[9] Kimmel hung up and hurried outside where he watched in anguish the destruction of

Arizona. Fewer than 200 of *Arizona*'s 1400-person crew survived the attack.

Nevada

Tied up near *Arizona*, the battleship *Nevada* was threatened by the *Arizona*'s flames. *Nevada* was also under attack from above. USS *Nevada*'s anti-aircraft battery returned fire under directions from twenty-one-year-old Ensign Joseph K. Taussig, Jr. Taussig's left leg had been shattered by a missile, but it did not stop him. After he shot down one torpedo plane, another plane successfully hit *Nevada*. The ship began to lean to one side, as water poured into the hole created by the torpedo. Below deck, the ship's crew flooded the other side of the ship and saved the *Nevada* from turning over on its side.

The senior officer on board the USS *Nevada*, Lieutenant Commander Francis Thomas, decided the ship should try to escape despite the flooding. Chief Boatswain Edwin J. Hill directed the casting-off of *Nevada*'s lines from the pier, then leapt in the water and swam back to his ship.[10] The *Nevada* started moving down the channel. A battleship normally needs a couple of hours to light its boilers, but fortunately Taussig had lit the boilers just before the attack. In this case the ship's two boilers enabled it to get steam up and start moving—without tugboats—past burning and sunken ships within forty-five minutes.

Japanese Commander Fuchida was circling above the harbor, taking pictures of the damage, when he saw the *Nevada* steaming out of Pearl Harbor. He quickly realized that if *Nevada* were sunk, the battleship would block the channel. As the second Japanese attack wave arrived, including seventy-eight dive bombers that were ordered to destroy all the ships that had survived the first wave. Many of the bombers swarmed down on the battleship. Thomas moved the USS *Nevada* out of the channel and onto Hospital Point, where he grounded it. As Chief Boatswain Hill went forward to drop anchor, three bombs dropped near the bow and he disappeared, never to be seen again. He was later awarded the Medal of Honor.[11]

West Virginia

While the *Tennessee* escaped with little damage, the nearby *West Virginia* was not so lucky. Captain Mervyn Bennion was on the signal bridge when he was maimed by a piece of flying metal from a bomb explosion. Mess Attendant Doris Miller, an African-American man who worked in the kitchen, was summoned to carry the captain to safety below, but flames blocked the way. Miller finally helped to carry him to a sheltered spot on the navigation bridge. Bennion did not want to leave the bridge. Still conscious, though near death, the captain insisted that his crew leave him and save themselves.

After putting the captain down, Doris Miller picked up a machine gun and began firing. He later helped Lieutenant (jg) Frederick White haul wounded men through oil and seawater, "unquestionably saving the lives of a number of people who might otherwise have been lost."[12] In 1941 the United States Navy only let African Americans serve as kitchen attendants. Miller was the first African American to win the Navy Cross and his heroic story helped end segregation in the Navy.

Oklahoma

When five torpedoes blasted into the battleship *Oklahoma*, there was no time to try to save the ship. Because the lower compartments had been left open for an expected inspection on Monday, the ship rapidly flooded. As men rushed to their battle stations in the darkness, *Oklahoma* capsized. Many of the crew members were trapped inside, but others escaped by climbing over the upturned hull.

As the ship turned over and the water in the compartments rose, many crewmen drowned. Lieutenant (jg) Aloysius Schmitt, a Catholic chaplain, started out a washroom porthole but a prayer book in his pocket caught in the frame. He backed away, and then others started through. Schmitt pushed four of them through the opening and was still in the compartment when water filled it completely. Schmitt was not the only one to sacrifice his own life to help others escape. Seaman James Ward and Ensign Francis Flaherty stayed inside a darkened gun turret as the vessel capsized and held flashlights so their shipmates could save themselves.

Many people tried to save the *Oklahoma* crew. Holes were cut in the sides of *Oklahoma* to rescue the trapped men. As the water rose, others tapped on the steel bulkhead with wrenches to draw attention. They hoped that by making noise, rescue workers would know where to cut the holes. The haunting tapping lasted for hours after the attack. Some people were rescued, but many others died in the ship.[13]

One survivor of the USS *Oklahoma*, Seaman Stephen B. Young, was certain that he would die. Young remembered the ire he felt: "Why couldn't we have died in the sun where we could have met

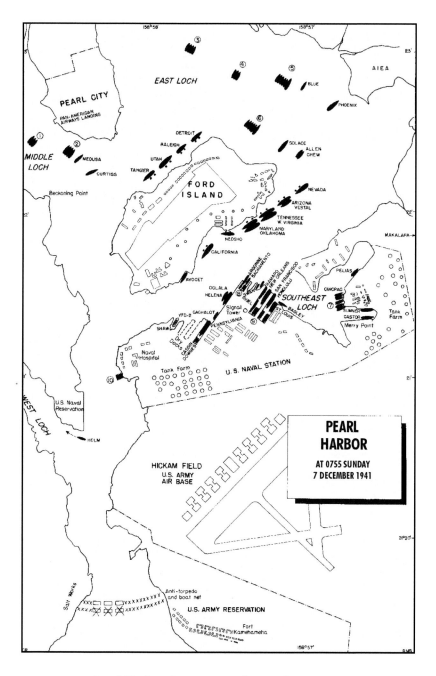

Pearl Harbor the morning of December 7, 1941

death head on? That was the way to die, on your feet, like a man."[14]

California

Several torpedoes struck *California* at 8:00 A.M., and ten minutes later the battleship's power went out. Water was pouring through the holes into the fuel tanks. In one flooded compartment Robert Scott was at his battle station at a compressor feeding air to *California*'s antiaircraft gun crew. Scott was ordered to leave but refused. "As long as I can give these people air, I'm sticking," he said. He did and it cost him his life.[15]

Herbert Jones set up a group to supply ammunition to *California*'s antiaircraft battery. Mortally wounded, he refused to be removed. Thomas Reeves also passed ammunition to the battery until he was killed. Jackson Pharris moved ammunition and pulled men to safety from the battery's flooded compartment. Badly injured and twice overcome by oil and fumes, he somehow survived—the only one of the four to do so. Scott, Jones, Reeves, and Pharris all won the Medal of Honor for their heroism that day.

The Airfields

The battleships were not the only targets for the Japanese attack. Japanese bombers attacked the nearby Kaneohe Naval Air Station, Hickam Field, Wheeler Field, Ewa Field, and Bellows Field. Bombers and fighter planes attacked these bases to stop Americans from launching a counterattack. As on the battleships, most people at these bases were completely surprised by the attack. At the Naval Air Station on Ford Island damage and casualties were relatively light because the combat planes were with their carriers at sea, but the other air fields were not so lucky.

Hickam Air Depot

Sixty-five bombers were based at Hickam Field. The bombers had been parked close together, neatly lined up so they could be more closely guarded against sabotage but helpless against an air attack. "There was confusion," one survivor recalled, "plus when the attack came men were completely petrified and frightened stiff."[16] Most of the bombers were destroyed. Hangars and barracks were attacked with gunfire from low-flying planes as well.

At Hickam, Robert Crouse and others awaited the arrival of the B-17s from California. At first

Crouse thought the smoke above the harbor came from a navy drill. But the planes flew in closer, and machine guns began firing. Bombs dropped. Some men with pistols shot vainly at the planes, others took cover. Crouse was wounded in the ankle and crawled into a hangar. It did not seem safe there so he got under a tractor until the first attack wave had gone. Then, bleeding badly, he dragged himself out and was picked up by a an American soldier using his car as an ambulance for four or five wounded men. A lieutenant aboard, Crouse recalled, "kept us amused by 'cussing' every bump and the driver alternately." Crouse met him again on a ship going back to the mainland and learned that the lieutenant who had sustained their spirits had lost both legs.[17]

A doctor at Hickam noticed that the clothing of Carmen Calderon, who had helped carry the wounded, was soaked in blood. The doctor insisted that Calderon undress for an examination. He found Calderon had been carrying the men with a broken arm. Hickam's casualties were the largest of any army post on that day: 158 dead or missing, 336 wounded.[18]

Wheeler

A United States fighter force of 140 planes was based at Wheeler Field in central Oahu. Just as at Hickam, all were parked close together so guards could protect them from possible sabotage. And just as at Hickam, they made an excellent target for the Japanese. At two minutes past 8:00 A.M., twenty-five dive bombers destroyed most of them. The bombers also attacked Schofield Barracks, the infantry post next to Wheeler, as well as tents where crewmen slept.

Kaneohe Naval Air Station

Kaneohe Naval Air Station endured three attacks. The first came at 7:45 A.M. as the marine guard was assembled for the morning flag-raising ceremony. Patrol planes, fueled, fully armed, and parked together, were set on fire. Eighteen more Japanese planes, most of them dive bombers, joined in the second attack. In the third attack, a bomb exploded in a hangar, killing several men trying to get ammunition stored there. As a result of all three attacks, every plane on the base was destroyed or badly damaged.

During the attack, John Finn, picked up a machine gun from one of the parked planes and began blazing away. Wounded in his stomach, chest, arms, and foot, he kept on firing until he was ordered to cease. "It was not my day to die," he said years later. "I was so hopping mad, I wanted to shoot every . . . plane out of the sky."[19] He, too, was awarded the Medal of Honor.

Ewa Field

Ewa Field was attacked by twenty Japanese fighters. After demolishing the aircraft on the field, they shot at personnel. Among the wounded was the base commander, Claude Larkin. Even after getting wounded, Larkin brought together the Ewa defenses, which consisted mostly of rifles and .30-caliber machine guns from damaged planes. A second attack at Ewa came at 8:35 A.M. and a third between 9 and 9:30 A.M. By the end, none of the forty-seven planes on the base could fly.

Bellows Field

Bellows Field, a small base a few miles southeast of Kaneohe, received phone calls from Hickam Field and from Kaneohe with reports of the attacks. In fact, Hickam had asked for and received fire fighting equipment from Bellows. So it is puzzling that when Bellows itself was attacked just before 8:30 A.M., no one was prepared. Private Raymond McBriarty saw a lone Japanese plane buzzing the field and continued on his way to chapel services. One of the B-17s from California, on its way to the Philippines, made a forced landing near the chapel, and at 9:00 A.M. about nine low-flying Japanese planes made a serious attack. The air raid signal finally sounded, and the chapel emptied as men rushed to their stations.

McBriarty picked up a gun, mounted it in a parked plane, and fired at the Japanese planes. When they left, he took off after them in the plane, but engine trouble forced him to abandon the chase.

One of the Bellows' officers, Phillip Willis, slept through the first attack, having returned just before dawn from an off-base party. The second attack woke him up. Still in his tuxedo trousers and shirt, he put on his helmet, flight jacket, and a pair of cowboy boots, and ran to the runway. When he got there, he saw a fighter pilot hampered by his parachute pack as he tried to climb into his cockpit. Willis ran to the plane to help the pilot. While there, Japanese machine-gun fire hit the plane and killed the pilot. Willis was saved by the parachute, which stopped the bullets from hitting him.[20]

Solace

To care for the many wounded, there were two hospitals ashore and a hospital ship in the harbor, *Solace*, which rapidly became an emergency ward. Nurses bathed and bandaged the wounded and helped the dying. They did not even look up when loudspeakers warned of enemy planes zooming above. The hospital ship was repeatedly rocked by bombs and nurses soon became covered with blood as they cared for the wounded amid the rat-a-tat-tat of machine guns and other weapons. It seemed that the Japanese were flying close to the hospital ship in an effort to protect themselves from the American antiaircraft fire.[21]

The nurses on *Solace* worked under Chief Nurse Grace Lally. Lally had been in the navy twenty years. In 1938 she had helped evacuate American women and children from China following the Japanese invasion. Seeing the courage of the wounded at Pearl Harbor, she was later determined that people on *Solace* would have a Christmas, with presents (from the Red Cross) and a decorated tree atop the mast. They did. In the first twenty months of the war in the Pacific, 7,500 casualties were treated aboard *Solace*. Only sixteen men died.[22]

Confused Friendly Fire

A little after 6:00 A.M. the aircraft carrier *Enterprise* sent eighteen American dive bombers to scout the area between his task force and Pearl Harbor. Later he was informed of the message from Ford Island about the raid.

"My God!" Admiral William Halsey exclaimed. "They're shooting at my own boys—tell [Admiral Husband] Kimmel!"[23]

Halsey's "boys" were indeed being shot at—by Japanese pilots as well as by confused Americans on the ground. One *Enterprise* pilot, Manuel Gonzales, shouted over the radio: "Don't shoot— I'm a friendly plane!" Gonzales and his plane were never seen again. Six *Enterprise* planes were shot down, at least one by American gunfire. Six others landed at Ewa Field, the Marine air base west of Pearl Harbor.[24]

The dozen B-17s on their way from California had been sent to help United States Army forces in the Philippines, under the command of General Douglas MacArthur. The planes were unarmed so that they could carry more fuel for the extensive fourteen-hour flight. The Hickam Field base commander had been waiting for them since 6:00 A.M. but they had been delayed by a navigation error.

They approached Oahu shortly after 8:00 A.M., completely unaware of the attack on Pearl Harbor.

As they did, Major Truman Landon, in command of the American planes, saw other planes flying toward him and assumed they were friendly. When he saw the rising sun on the wings he immediately knew something was wrong. "Those are Japs!" he shouted over his intercom.[25]

Many Americans on the ground, thinking the American planes were part of the Japanese attack, fired at them. But somehow all the American bombers managed to land, although several were in bad shape and one was destroyed.

Chapter 5

A DEVASTATING LOSS

One of the duties of the Japanese flight leader was to assess the damage at Pearl Harbor for a report to Admiral Chuichi Nagumo, who headed the strike force. Commander Fuchida rejoiced at the task. Through the heavy smoke he had counted seven battleships sunk or badly damaged, a cruiser crippled, all the Hawaiian airfields in flames, and almost no American aircraft in the skies.

The toll was more devastating than Fuchida realized. Five battleships were sunk and three others had been heavily damaged. Three cruisers and six auxiliary vessels were badly damaged, and four destroyers put out of action. A total of twenty-one vessels were sunk or damaged. Only the navy's submarines survived the attack undamaged.

The ships at Pearl Harbor, at least, fought back. Most of the planes did not: they were parked on the ground, wingtip to wingtip. Admiral Kimmel and General Short believed that was the best way to guard against sabotage. As a result, the airplanes were easy targets for the Japanese attack. Based on some estimates, the Navy lost eighty planes—more than half its total in Hawaii. Of 234 Army aircraft, 97 were written off as lost.

The toll in American lives was also high, although no one is sure exactly how many died. The Navy and Marine Corps apparently had 3,077 killed, 960 missing, and 876 wounded. The Army casualties were 226 killed and 396 wounded. Most of the Navy and Marine dead were on the *Arizona*, as were most of the missing. In one day, the Navy lost three times as many men as it had lost from enemy action in two previous wars—the Spanish-American War and World War I.[1]

There were many wounded. The staff at Pearl Harbor Naval Hospital treated 545 battle casualties, 350 of them with extensive body burns. At the Army's Tripler General Hospital at Fort Shafter, the wives and daughters of servicemen helped treat the patients, as did civilian employees and civilian doctors and nurses.

Civilians, in fact, were quite well prepared for disaster: Honolulu officials had established the Major Disaster Council in June 1941 to handle crises. The council had set up a system using private trucks as emergency ambulances.

Japanese losses were relatively minor. One dive bomber, five torpedo planes, and three fighters were lost in the first wave. Six fighters and fourteen dive bombers were shot down from the second wave, when the defenders were somewhat better prepared. Only fifty-five Japanese airmen were lost in action.

Fuchida was eager to attack again. He wanted another crack at the airfields and a chance to sink more ships. He appealed to Nagumo to allow him to lead a third air strike. Nagumo, however, worried about the American's ability to counterattack. Where were the absent aircraft carriers? Both Fuchida and Nagumo realized these ships could be pursuing the Japanese strike force. In fact, the American aircraft carrier, *Enterprise*, was searching for the Japanese fleet. Nagumo believed his mission had been accomplished. Why risk bigger losses? When Fuchida realized there would be no third raid, he saluted the admiral without speaking and walked off angrily.[2]

The decision not to attack again spared the Navy's ship repair shops and oil tanks. Fuchida noticed these targets, but he did not bomb them. Destruction of the shops and tanks would have made the American defeat far greater. The oil tanks held 4.5 million gallons. After the war Admiral Kimmel testified that if they had been destroyed, "It would have forced the withdrawal of the fleet to the coast."[3] The tanks' loss, according to Commander Edwin T. Layton, Kimmel's intelligence officer, would have kept the American carrier forces from operating in the western Pacific for more than six months.

The intact repair shops enabled the Navy to do an outstanding job of restoring most of the damaged ships under conditions that were incredibly difficult and dangerous. A combination of fuel oil and seawater flooded most of the sunken battleships, making it necessary for repair workers to spend twenty thousand hours underwater.[4]

Because it would be months before ships then under construction in California and elsewhere could be completed, speed in repairs was essential. One remarkable example was *Nevada*. Lieutenant Commander Francis Thomas had intentionally grounded that battleship when it was under attack. His action kept the harbor channel open, allowing the Navy to continue using Pearl Harbor. The ship was almost entirely flooded and hydrogen sulfide, a deadly gas, had accumulated in the steering engine room, killing two men and overcoming six others.

Nevada was refloated on February 12 and before the end of 1942 was back in service. Of the other battleships, *California* was restored to duty in 1943, and *West Virginia* joined the war effort in 1944. Sadly, much time and money were spent on *Oklahoma* before it was decided it could not be rehabilitated. *Oklahoma* was finally sold as scrap metal in 1944. While being towed to the mainland it sank at sea in a storm.[5]

Utah and *Arizona* still rest at the bottom of Pearl Harbor. A memorial spanning *Arizona*'s hull was built in 1962. Those who have visited the memorial have found it a moving experience.

Luck, both good and bad, played a part in the Pearl Harbor disaster. Because some B-17s were flying toward Oahu at the same time as the Japanese fighter planes, the radar blip betraying the attackers was disregarded. And a last-minute alert sent by The Chief of Staff, General George Marshall to both Short and Kimmel before the attack did not arrive until long after it had begun, for a variety of mischances.

Destiny — or luck — may have played a part in still another circumstance: the location of the American battleships. They could all have been at sea, where Kimmel had considered sending them a short time before the attack. Had the battleships been discovered and attacked in deeper waters, their sinking would have been a calamity. "It was God's divine will," Admiral Chester Nimitz, who replaced Kimmel as Pacific Fleet commander, said later.[6]

Chapter 6

THE AFTERMATH

Immediately after the attack on Oahu, anger and determination were mixed with confusion and fear. Rumors quickly spread that the Japanese would invade Hawaii. The loyalty of the territory's 160,000 Japanese residents came immediately into question.

At the Punahou elementary school, there were American and Japanese students. One American, Martha Branneman, remembered one Japanese teacher—Mr. Wattanbe—as "wonderful." The children—Japanese as well as the non-Japanese— continued to play together after the attack, she recalled in an atmosphere of "genuine caring for each other."[1]

General Short, however, warned Hawaii's governor, Joseph B. Poindexter, that uprisings by

Japanese residents were likely. The general persuaded Poindexter to proclaim martial law over all Hawaii, putting the army in control of all aspects of civilian life. Schools were closed and the sale of liquor was banned for months.

The day after the attack "Japanese paratroopers" in dungarees were reported to have landed on Oahu. At the Kaneohe Air Station, sailors were ordered to change from dungarees into whites dyed (with coffee) a deep brown. Then came a corrected report: The invaders wore khakis, change to whites. Next came another report: The invaders wore white. A new order followed: All hands, back to dungarees![2]

That evening, John Garcia, a young Hawaiian worker at the Pearl Harbor Navy Yard, drove a truckload of marines a few miles into the valley where the Japanese paratroopers were said to have landed. A total blackout, ordered by authorities, was in effect. Suddenly the lights went on at a house in the valley and the marines started shooting at it. The lights quickly went out. There were no paratroopers.

On the mainland, the feeling in some areas, especially on the West Coast, was not far from panic. Three air-raid alerts were sounded in San Francisco on the night after the attack. Mayor

Fiorello LaGuardia of New York warned of the possibility of an attack on the East Coast.

War Declared

On December 8, President Franklin D. Roosevelt asked Congress for a declaration of war against Japan. His five-minute speech was aired nationwide over the radio. Few of the millions who heard it ever forgot it. Both houses of Congress approved the war declaration with only one vote against war.

Before Pearl Harbor, many Americans opposed involvement in a war. The "sneak attack" by Japan changed things. The nation was swept by a wave of patriotism. It would be an exaggeration to say that the isolationist movement died overnight, but it came close to just that. One prominent isolationist, former President Herbert Hoover, said shortly after the attack: "American soil has been treacherously attacked by Japan. Our decision is clear. It is forced upon us. We must fight with everything we have."[3] It was a demonstration of the sudden change in mood caused by the attack. Newspapers across the country expressed anger and determination to fight.[4]

At the time of Pearl Harbor there were a million and a half men in the United States Army, and a million of them were still in training.

To thousands of young men hearing about the attack there was no doubt about what to do. They went directly to a service headquarters to enlist. Sometimes they joined a line several blocks long. Many were told they already had a draft notice from the president of the United States informing them they were to be inducted into the army.

One of these men, Elliot Johnson of Portland, Oregon, soon found himself in a new world where discipline was the key word. But he was happy because "we were fighting to save the free world and keep it free."[5]

More than fifteen million men served in the United States armed forces during World War II. More than 300,000 of them were killed, including 36,000 in the Navy and 19,000 in the Marine Corps. In contrast, 1.2 million Japanese servicemen were killed in battle.

Following the attack on Pearl Harbor everything changed. "There was a complete change in attitude," said William Pefley who worked at the navy yard in Portsmouth, Virginia. "We weren't just helping England [fight against Germany] anymore; we were helping ourselves. Now it was our war. So everybody decided: 'No matter what the hours may be, let's get the ships out. Whatever we can do to help this war effort, we are going to do.'"[6]

Two days after the attack President Roosevelt delivered his second radio address about the issue. Roosevelt warned that America faced a great challenge. To meet that challenge, the president said, the American people would have to live with many shortages. Gasoline, sugar, meat, and other things would have to be rationed. Higher taxes, smaller profits, longer working hours, and dangerous duty in the army and navy lay ahead.[7]

War in Europe

On December 11, Germany declared war on the United States of America. Winston Churchill, the British Prime Minister, was relieved to know that the United States would now help fight against Germany. Great Britain needed more than just American supplies, Great Britain also needed American soldiers. The need for a conference seemed urgent, so Churchill came to Washington on December 22, 1941, and stayed for three weeks. The United States joined Great Britain and the other "Allied" countries in their fight against Germany, Italy, and Japan. American defeats continued in the Pacific. The need for more ships, planes, and munitions in the Pacific concerned the president, but he also promised to help the British defeat the Germans President Franklin Roosevelt and Churchill had been friends for several years, but were now closer than ever. Churchill telegraphed from the White House: "We live here as a big family in the greatest intimacy and informality, and I have formed the very highest regard and admiration for the president." As a consequence of their friendship, the wartime alliance between the two nations became extraordinarily effective.[8]

Boom on the Home Front

After Pearl Harbor, the government spent vast sums of money to buy new weapons for the military. The entire auto business was converted to the production of munitions. This caused forty-four thousand auto dealers and their four hundred thousand employees to be laid off. However, plenty of jobs were available and unemployment all but vanished. New defense factories sprang up across the country like mushrooms. Older plants were put to new use. A corset factory began making grenade belts. A factory that was making pinball machines now produced armor-piercing shells. In aircraft plants, farm girls learned how to rivet, and at navy yards they learned how to weld. Five million women joined the civilian work force from 1941 to 1943. The total work force increased by

7 million during the war, to more than 53 million in 1945.

Early in January, Roosevelt warned Congress and the people in his State of the Union message that "the news is going to get worse and worse before it begins to get better," and that he would have to ask again for sacrifices. New production goals had to be set. Those he listed for 1942 included: 60,000 planes, 45,000 tanks, 20,000 antiaircraft guns, 6 million tons of merchant shipping. These figures, considered astronomical then, "will give the Japanese and the Nazis a little idea of just what they accomplished at Pearl Harbor," President Roosevelt said as Congress cheered.[9]

New military bases were rapidly built, and millions of families moved to cramped production centers. Shantytowns sprang up. There were so few beds in some places that they were rented out in three shifts a day. Eventually, however, defense factory workers got $100 million worth of new housing.

Workers' wages, boosted by overtime, came to far exceed what they had previously been a short time earlier. William Pefley recalled: "Going to work in the navy yard after coming out of the machine shops in Pennsylvania, I felt like something had come down from heaven. I went from forty cents an hour to a dollar an hour." Like many, Pefley was driven by more than simply the desire to increase his pay: "[I]t was very important that we got every single ship that came in [for repairs] out quickly so they'd be fighting again. . . . Many a time the men would work eight hours and you needed some of them, the experienced ones, to get the ship out on time. So we'd ask who would care to work straight through. And just about every-body there would volunteer and work until they could almost go to sleep. . . . Your best friend might be out there on one of those ships, maybe getting bombed."[10]

Difficult living conditions, supply shortages, high taxes all brought grumbles, which were met with the universal rejoinder "Don't you know there's a war on?" The result of all the effort was that America produced more than 300,000 planes, 87,000 warships, 102,000 tanks, and 47 million tons of artillery ammunition.

Suspicion on Both Sides

After the attack on Pearl Harbor, many Americans worried about the threat of sabotage posed by Japanese Americans. Everyone was caught up in the suspicion. After seeing Pearl Harbor for him-self, Secretary of the Navy Frank Knox said he believed the attack had succeeded largely because of sabotage. No evidence of sabotage was ever found.

Suspicion of Japanese and Japanese Americans was high throughout the war. The *Los Angeles Times* put it this way: "A viper is nonetheless a viper wherever the egg is hatched—so a Japanese-American, born of Japanese parents, grows up to be a Japanese, not an American."[11]

Finally, in 1942, President Roosevelt decided to send 110,000 Japanese Americans to live in "detention centers." More than seventy thousand were American citizens. The homes, jobs, and property of these people were taken away and they were forced to live in ten fenced-in prison camps. The living quarters were in tar-papered wooden barracks containing one-room apartments furnished with cots, blankets, and a light bulb. Meals were unpleasant and there was little medical care. In one case, two thousand Japanese Americans were kept in a single building in a stockyard in Portland, Oregon, sleeping there on sacks filled with straw.[12]

THE WAR IN THE PACIFIC

For the United States and its allies, the first six months of the war in the Pacific were dark indeed as Japan won a series of quick and impressive victories. The Japanese were exultant. After making little progress in a war with China, suddenly the Japanese controlled a wide area in the South Pacific. Their visions of building a string of bases across the Pacific so strong that the United States and Australia would not dare attack them seemed possible.

After their successful attack on Pearl Harbor, the Japanese focused attention on the United States bases in the Philippines. The Philippines were a group of more than 7,000 islands that stretched over 1,100 miles across the western Pacific ocean. From the Philippines, the Japanese planned to take control of much of Southeast Asia and nearby Pacific islands. This area had rich supplies of oil, rubber and tin. These were extremely important materials for the Japanese military. The Japanese hoped that taking control of this area would also protect them from attack by the United States.

The Japanese believed that after they had taken over Southeast Asia and the Pacific the United States might be willing to negotiate. They believed that the United States would not want to fight in the Pacific Ocean after losing so many of its ships during the attack at Pearl Harbor. Japan falsely believed the United States would not be committed to fighting the war.[1]

The Philippines

Less than nine hours after the attack on Pearl Harbor, Japanese planes bombed Clark Field on the island of Luzon, in the Philippines. They demolished about one hundred of MacArthur's planes, all parked on the ground. The effectiveness of the United States Far Eastern Air Force was destroyed. The United States had controlled the Philippines since 1898, but now faced a Japanese invasion with few soldiers, ships, or planes.

Disaster followed disaster. On December 10, Japanese invaders landed on Luzon. Luzon is the biggest island in the Philippines and had the biggest city, Manila. American troops fought hard to save Manila. Faced with overwhelming numbers, Americans evacuated Manila and retreated to Bataan at the tip of the island. Finally, on April 9, 1942, after four months of fighting, the Americans surrendered. By June 9, all Philippine resistance to the Japanese had ended.

The Japanese were extremely cruel to their prisoners. After their surrender, American and Filipino prisoners were forced to march one hundred miles in what became notorious as the Bataan Death March. During the march 10,650 men died. In prison camp, 17,600 more died.

More Japanese Victories

Japanese forces swiftly conquered Hong Kong, and the islands of Borneo and Malaya. The Japanese also forced the Allies to retreat in Burma, now called Thailand. Capturing the American islands of Guam on December 10 and Wake on December 22 gave Japan still more important bases.

The Japanese continued to have success after success during the early months of 1942. The Japanese military defeated the Allies, taking big cities like Hong Kong and Singapore as well as important islands like Guam, New Guinea, and Java. These victories helped Japan take control of Southeast Asia and the western Pacific.

The Doolittle Raid

On the morning of April 18, 1942, the startled crew of a Japanese fishing boat 720 miles east of Tokyo saw an American naval force steaming westward. The fishermen immediately radioed Yamamoto's headquarters. The fishermen spotted Admiral William Halsey's task force, including the carrier *Hornet*, transporting sixteen long-range B-25 Army bombers—larger than normal carrier planes. The B-25s, under Lieutenant Col. James Doolittle, were to launch within five hundred miles of the coast, bomb Tokyo, and fly to China.

Halsey saw the fishing boat. Deciding not to put the carriers in peril by moving closer to the coast, Halsey ordered an immediate launching. An attack from that distance was not expected and the bombers met almost no opposition. They caused little damage, but the Japanese were humiliated: the sanctity of their homeland had been violated and it would not have happened had the fleet's carriers been at Pearl Harbor on December 7.

After all their initial successes, the Japanese were unsure how to proceed. Admiral Isoroku Yamamoto believed the capture of Midway, 1,136 miles west of Pearl Harbor, was a necessary preliminary to a Hawaii invasion. He thought he could lure the United States forces into battle there and defeat them, thus shortening the war—the only way he thought Japan could win.[2]

The Doolittle raid ended the opposition in Japan to an attack on Midway. It would surely bring out United States naval forces in full, the Japanese believed, and they were confident they could win and be in a position to invade Hawaii. At any rate, they could add another island to their defensive chain.

On May 23 Imperial Headquarters ordered training to begin for the invasion of Hawaii. But first, of course, they had to seize Midway. That battle began on June 4.

Midway: The Japanese Are Halted

Admiral Yamamoto had hoped to destroy the United States Pacific Fleet at Midway. He instead suffered a stunning defeat. His complex plan called for part of his force to be sent to the western Aleutians, between Alaska and Japan, to confuse the Americans and to obtain defensive bases. He did not confuse anyone; American code breakers learned about his plans.

The division of Japanese forces contributed to a United States victory at Midway. The aircraft carriers that had escaped the Pearl Harbor disaster were another factor. Japan lost four aircraft carriers, three hundred planes, hundreds of expert air crews and a heavy cruiser, while the United States lost one carrier and a destroyer. Yamamoto's force still had several carriers and a large surface fleet, but for the Allies, the tide had begun to turn. General George Marshall, the chief of staff, said later: "The closest squeak and the greatest victory [in the Pacific] was at Midway."[3]

Midway ended Japan's plan to invade Hawaii. Australia, though, was another matter. That island continent was a rapidly increasing source of Allied manpower and military production, as American forces rapidly headed there. One good place from which to bomb Australia was Rabaul, which the Japanese had seized in January 1942. Another possible base for air strikes was Port Moresby, an Allied base in New Guinea, which the Japanese hoped to seize. After Midway, on the unoccupied island of Guadalcanal, the Japanese began to build a major air base.

Retaking the South Pacific

Japan and the United States focused on New Guinea and the Solomon Islands, an island chain six hundred miles long. Both New Guinea and the Solomon Islands are located between Hawaii and Australia. In the next year and a half, thousands died over these islands in some of the most savage fighting of the war.

General Douglas MacArthur was now in command of the Allied forces in the Southwest Pacific. MacArthur wanted to return to the Philippines and then move on to Japan. On July 2, 1942, the United States began a two-pronged advance on New Guinea and the Solomon Islands. Admiral Chester Nimitz led an attack on the Japanese in the Solomon Islands. At the same time, MacArthur led a force that attacked the Japanese in the jungles of New Guinea.

The plan was initiated when a force of United States Marines landed on Guadalcanal, one of the Solomon Islands. Japanese soldiers building an air base on Guadalcanal were completely surprised. The epic struggle for the 2,250 square-mile island of Guadalcanal involved ships and planes as well as ground forces, and there were no easy times for anyone on land, sea, or air. Fear and fatigue were constant. In the jungle, disease was as big a challenge as the opposing troops. Mosquitoes bearing malaria seemed deadlier than the enemy.

Ground combat was probably the worst ordeal. A marine sergeant had this memory long afterward:

> The real battle for Guadalcanal was in October [1942]. Both sides built up, and got in the middle of the ring. They wanted the airport and we wanted to hold it at all cost. That was it. They sent in ships, planes, everything.... It was the second night of the battle. There had been heavy action down the line. After all the noise earlier it was so quiet you could hear the men breathing.... I moved along the line warning the men not to fire yet but to let the Japs get close and then give them everything.... We heard soft muttering down in the jungle....[S] omeone shrieked and all hell let loose.... It was a confusing struggle lit up by flashes from machine-gun fire.... In the flickering light I saw three Japanese charge.... I shot two of them, but the third ran through one of my gunners with a bayonet and actually lifted him into the air. I shot him too.[4]

On the island of New Guinea, meanwhile, Japanese and American troops fought a "war of annihilation." Both sides also fought disease in jungles, swamps, and eight-foot tall kunai grass.[5]

Every infantryman carried hand grenades. Each contained two ounces of TNT that could be thrown one hundred feet. They were used frequently on bunkers containing Japanese, who "had a habit of throwing our grenades back so we had to hold a four-second grenade for two or three seconds before hurling it."[6]

In September 1942 American air strikes and Australian ground troops forced the Japanese to halt their drive to Port Moresby, in New Guinea. On February 7, 1943, the last Japanese troops were forced to leave Guadalcanal, ending the long nightmare there. Many difficult battles lay ahead in the Pacific, but the Japanese army had been forced to stop.

Closing In

Following the victory at Guadalcanal, Japanese and American troops fought over many more islands in the Pacific Ocean. The United States won victory after victory, but often at great cost. On the Island of Tarawa in the central Pacific, 4,500 Japanese and 1,300 Americans were killed. More than two thousand more Americans were wounded in the battle. Step by step, American forces moved closer and closer to Japan. The United States wanted to get close to Japan to build airports for the new B-29 Superfortress airplanes. Finally, Americans defeated the Japanese at the island of Saipan, on June 15 1944. Saipan was only 1,200 miles from Tokyo. The American victory at Saipan meant that B-29s could now easily drop bombs on Japan.

Another important step for the American military was to re-take the Philippines. Before leaving the Philippine islands in 1942, General MacArthur vowed to return.

MacArthur finally got his chance to return. "They are waiting for me there—it has been a long time," said MacArthur.[7] In October 1944, the United States and Japanese navies faced each other in an epic sea battle at Leyte Gulf. Leyte was one of the Philippine Islands, and the Japanese knew they must win to have any long-term chance against the Americans. Using every weapon they could, the Japanese fought ferociously. A Japanese suicide weapon called "kamikaze" was introduced in Leyte Gulf. Planes were turned into human missiles as pilots crashed them into enemy ships. Even kamikazes were not enough to turn the tide. Despite high casualties, the Americans defeated the Japanese and destroyed four aircraft carriers, three battleships, and nineteen destroyers.

After the Leyte Gulf naval battle, in October 1944, United States troops landed on Leyte itself. Unexpectedly bitter fighting delayed a landing on the main Philippine island of Luzon until January. American troops reached Manila in February, but over 12,000 Americans died, along with 16,000 Japanese and 100,000 Filipinos. The Philippines struggle finally ended on March 2, 1945. Douglas MacArthur had returned and conquered.

The Final Steps

Battle after battle, the American troops closed in on Japan. The island of Iwo Jima, 750 miles from central Japan, was next. The Japanese had built two airstrips on its volcanic soil and were beginning a third when the American troops landed early in February 1945. The attack was not unexpected and the Japanese fire that greeted it was vast and deadly, day and night. The fighting did not end until the end of March. Of the Marines who landed there, 6,821 were killed and 20,000 wounded. Nearly all the 21,000 Japanese defenders died in the fighting.

The Japanese were also prepared for an attack on the next island—Okinawa—400 miles closer to Japan. In the fighting from the April 1 landing, until the resistance ended on June 21, up to

120,000 Japanese troops and 170,000 civilians perished while 12,000 Americans were killed and over 33,000 were wounded.

Three days after the American victory at Iwo Jima, President Franklin Delano Roosevelt died on March 29, 1945. Roosevelt was the only president to be elected four times and had served as president through the Great Depression, Pearl Harbor, and most of World War II. Now the world's attention turned to his little-known vice president, Harry S Truman. Would Roosevelt's death affect the American military? Roosevelt had guided America through difficult times and nobody knew whether Truman would display the same kind of leadership.

The problems confronting Truman would not be easy. In view of the high number of casualties at Iwo Jima, Americans worried about what would happen with an invasion of Japan. United States military leaders had been instructed to plan an invasion. A landing on the mountainous island of Kyushu was scheduled for November 1945, and another landing on the main island of Honshu for March, 1946.

While the Japanese had been steadily forced to give ground, it was clear that they would keep on fighting, mainly because of the Allies' policy of demanding "unconditional surrender." This meant that the Allies—the United States, Britain, and the Soviet Union—would dictate the terms of the surrender. There was no guarantee that the Japanese could keep their emperor, and so they fought all the harder.

Meanwhile, polls in the United States in the summer of 1945 showed that most Americans wanted revenge on Japanese Emperor Hirohito. Anger from the attack on Pearl Harbor had festered for four years. The anger was intensified by reports of extreme Japanese cruelty, some of which became public knowledge only after the war. Examples of these were biological experiments on humans and the dropping of "plague" bombs on Chinese cities to see if the Japanese could start outbreaks of disease. Also, during the war one million Koreans were brought to Japan to work as "virtual slaves."[8]

There were exceptions to the brutal treatment. One American woman held in a camp in the Philippines wrote of the relationship between Japanese guards and American prisoners, "They really liked each other."[9]

For many, Japanese brutality was common. Some reports were false, but the true incidents were awful enough. They included "wounded

Japanese using hidden hand grenades to kill their rescuers and themselves" and Americans captured on Guadalcanal whose livers were removed by a Japanese doctor without pain killers. The Japanese announced that as a matter of policy the crews of B-29 bombers who bailed out over Japan or who crashed at sea would be killed.[10]

The most Japanese prisoners held at one time by Americans was 5,424, of whom slightly over one percent died. The Japanese captured 95,000 Allied servicemen. More than one out of every three American prisoners of war held by the Japanese—nearly 38 percent—perished, many of them horribly.

The Japanese were not alone in treating their enemy with contempt. The feeling that Japanese were subhuman was common among American servicemen. A general remembered, "Killing a Japanese was like killing a rattlesnake. I didn't always have that feeling in Europe about some poor German family man, but I felt with a Jap it was like killing a rattlesnake."[11]

Before sending troops to Japan, America started long-distance bombing raids. General Curtis LeMay decided to send B-29 bombers with no guns so they could carry even more bombs. On March 9, 1945, loaded up with firebombs, B-29 bombers destroyed 16 square miles of Tokyo and left over a million homeless and 87,000 dead.

More bombing raids followed on Tokyo and other cities: 520 B-29s hit Tokyo on May 23 and 564 two days later; 450 hit Yokohama on the 29th; 599 hit Osaka and Nagoya on July 24. The attacks killed at least 241,000 and left 313,000 injured.

Despite the high casualties, Japan still did not surrender. The United States did have another option. For years, American scientists had been working to create an atomic bomb. This bomb would be much more powerful than any other bomb ever built. Finally, on July 16, 1945, they succeeded in testing the world's first atomic bomb. Deciding to use the bomb, however, was not an easy decision. President Truman described the atomic bomb in his diary as "the most terrible thing ever discovered."[12] Many people, including the well-known scientist, Albert Einstein, believed the bomb was too horrible to ever use. Still, Truman and many others hoped the bomb would help to end the war and save American lives that would be lost were the United States to invade Japan.

On August 6, at about 8:15 A.M. (Japanese time), a B-29 at 30,000 feet released the bomb, which exploded 1,900 feet above Hiroshima and destroyed most of the city. The exact number of deaths cannot be measured, but nearly 100,000 were instantly killed. Recent surveys give 130,000 as the total killed, including those who died from acute exposure to radiation.

On August 8, 1.5 million Soviet troops invaded Manchuria and joined the war against Japan. A day later, a second atomic bomb was dropped on Nagasaki causing a death toll of between sixty and seventy thousand.

In Japan the emperor and his advisors, civilian and military, held two emotional conferences on the ninth and fourteenth of August. The militarist and peace factions remained divided, but it finally became clear to all that the only option to ending the war was suicidal resistance. On August 14 the Emperor signed a decree. It did not contain the word "surrender," but it ended the war.

Surrender and Occupation

In Tokyo Bay on the morning of September 2, 1945, aboard Admiral Nimitz's flagship, the battleship *Missouri*, an ordinary mess table covered with a green cloth was set up on the admiral's veranda deck. On the USS *Missouri* Japan's surrender was accepted by General MacArthur, the newly named supreme commander of the Allied Forces in Japan.

A few days after the signing, MacArthur established headquarters in the United States Embassy in Tokyo. An American flag that had flown in Washington on the day of Pearl Harbor, and on *Missouri* during the surrender, was raised on the embassy flagpole. Japan was in chaos. Air raids had killed 670,000 of the 1,850,000 Japanese who had died in the war and many cities lay in ruins. There was very little food or clothing.

The Allied occupation of Japan was peaceful from the start, perhaps because people on both sides desperately wanted peace. One of them was Commander Mitsuo Fuchida, who had led the air attack on Pearl Harbor. Fuchida became a small farmer in his home town.

The news that the war was finally over caused jubilation all over America. One who did not celebrate was Signalman First Class Lee Ebner, who was on board the battleship *West Virginia* when the bombs fell at Pearl Harbor. Later he served on other ships in combat. When word came of the war's end, Ebner was on a ship in Subic Bay in the Philippines. He did not join other sailors as they jumped for joy. All he could think of was his friends who were not there, and the destruction he had seen. He "just sat down and rested his chin in his hands and stared at the deck."[13]

Chapter 8

THE LEGACY OF PEARL HARBOR

For Americans, World War II began at Pearl Harbor and ended at Nagasaki.

Many Americans remembered exactly where they were when they heard about the attack on Pearl Harbor. It became an important event that divided time. Before Pearl Harbor was the Great Depression, a time of high unemployment, poverty, and little hope. After Pearl Harbor was World War II. The war ended the Great Depression and brought Americans together to defeat Germany and Japan.

By ending the Great Depression, Pearl Harbor did what America could not do alone. For twelve years Americans struggled during the Depression. Many, many Americans were unemployed, poor, and hungry during this period. After his first election, in 1932, President Roosevelt enacted many programs to end the Depression—but it still continued.

Suddenly on December 8, 1941, America needed to rebuild its Navy and prepare for war against Germany and Japan. For the first time since the Great Depression began, there were nearly enough jobs for everybody. Many American men enlisted in the army and navy. Some other men and many women found jobs to aid the war effort. American workers built new airplanes and ships, and rebuilt the ships damaged at Pearl Harbor.

Pearl Harbor also changed American attitudes toward foreign wars. Before Pearl Harbor many Americans were isolationists. Famous people like aviator Charles Lindbergh and former President Herbert Hoover opposed the war. Many in the United States heard of the horrible actions of Nazi Germany as they attacked Poland, France, and other countries, but they still did not want to fight the Germans. After bombs dropped on Hawaii, few people opposed involvement in World War II. The United States had been attacked and needed to defend itself. Before Pearl Harbor, entering the war seemed unthinkable. After the Pearl Harbor attack, Americans joined the war effort with gusto.

The bombing of Pearl Harbor also made many Americans suspicious of people of Japanese ancestry living in the United States. In the wake of Pearl Harbor, Japanese Americans and Japanese citizens living in the western United States faced violence and discrimination. In western states where many lived, all people of Japanese ancestry—even natural born American citizens—came under suspicion. In February 1942, President Roosevelt ordered that "enemy aliens" be sent to internment camps. Japanese Americans lost their jobs, homes, and almost everything they owned and were forced into cramped prison camps. Many Japanese and Japanese-Americans remained in these camps for years until nearly the end of the war.

Perhaps the most lasting impact of the bombing of Pearl Harbor is on the survivors and the families and friends of American soldiers who died that day. Since the attack, they have worked to keep the memory of Pearl Harbor alive and to honor those who died there. In 1960, the USS *Arizona* Memorial opened at Pearl Harbor floating above the wreckage of the *Arizona* battleship. The memorial serves as a reminder of the sacrifice of all the men and women who died in the attack and especially the thousand crew members who died on the *Arizona*.

☆ TIMELINE ☆

1931—*September 18*: Japan invades Manchuria, a region of China. Some historians consider the invasion of Manchuria to be the actual start of World War II.

1941—*September 22*: Japanese invade French Indochina. In response the United States stops selling oil to Japan.

November 11: Japanese fleet leaves for Pearl Harbor.

November 27: United States Department of War issues a "war warning" to all U.S. military bases.

December 1: Japanese military officials make the final decision to attack Pearl Harbor.

December 7, 4:35 A.M. (Hawaiian time): Japanese submarine spotted near Pearl Harbor.

December 7, 6:15 A.M.: The first wave of Japanese airplanes takes off from Japanese carrier fleet.

December 7, 7:02 A.M.: Japanese airplanes spotted by American radar operators.

December 7, 7:03 A.M.: Japanese submarine sunk just outside the entrance to Pearl Harbor.

December 7, 7:56 A.M.: First wave of attack on Pearl Harbor begins.

December 22: Japan invades Philippines.

1942—*February 19*: President Franklin Roosevelt signs Executive Order 9066, allowing the military to relocate Japanese and Japanese Americans living in the United States.

April 18: James Doolittle leads American bombing raid on Tokyo.

June 4: United States bests Japan in Battle of Midway.

1943—*February 8*: United States wins Battle of Guadalcanal.

1944—*October 21*: General MacArthur returns to the Philippines.

December: Relocation and internment of Japanese and Japanese Americans ends.

1945—*April 12*: President Franklin Roosevelt dies. Harry S Truman becomes president.

July 16: First atomic bomb test in New Mexico.

August 6: United States drops first atomic bomb on Hiroshima, Japan.

August 9: United States drops the second atomic bomb on Nagasaki, Japan.

September 2: Japan surrenders to allies and ends World War II.

1988—*August 4*: The Civil Rights Bill of 1988 contains a formal apology to Japanese and Japanese Americans interned at camps during World War II.

☆ CHAPTER NOTES ☆

Introduction

1. Gordon W. Prange in collaboration with Donald M. Goldstein and Katherine V. Dillon, *At Dawn We Slept: The Untold Story of Pearl Harbor* (New York: Viking Penguin, 1981), pp. 406–411.

2. Prange, *At Dawn We Slept*, p. 97.

Chapter 1. The Day Before

1. Gordon W. Prange with Donald M. Goldstein and Katherine V. Dillon, *December 7 1941: The Day the Japanese Attacked Pearl Harbor* (New York: McGraw Hill, 1988), pp. 41–42.

2. Gordon W. Prange in collaboration with Donald M. Goldstein and Katherine V. Dillon, *At Dawn We Slept: The Untold Story of Pearl Harbor* (New York: Viking Penguin, 1981), pp. 73–75.

3. Walter Lord, *Day of Infamy* (New York: Bantam, 1958), pp. 6–7.

4. Lord, *Day of Infamy*, pp. 7–9; Prange, *December 7*, pp. 35–41, 79.

Chapter 2. War or Peace?

1. John Toland, *The Rising Sun: the Decline and Fall of the Japanese Empire 1936-1945*, Vol. 1 (New York: Random House, 1970), p. 114.

2. David C. Evans and Mark R. Peattie, *Kaigun: Strategy, Tactics and Technology in the Imperial Japanese Navy 1887-1941* (Annapolis: Naval Institute Press, 1997), p. 606.

3. Gordon W. Prange in collaboration with Donald M. Goldstein and Katherine V. Dillon, *At Dawn We Slept: The Untold Story of Pearl Harbor* (New York: Viking Penguin, 1981), pp. 98–106.

4. Alvin D. Coox, "The Pearl Harbor Raid Revisited," *The Journal of American–East Asian Relations* (Fall 1994), p. 217; Prange, *At Dawn We Slept*, p. 445.

5. Walter Lord, *Day of Infamy* (New York: Bantam, 1958), p. 25.

6. Prange, *At Dawn We Slept*, p. 487.

Chapter 3. Early Warnings

1. Gordon W. Prange in collaboration with Donald M. Goldstein and Katherine V. Dillon, *At Dawn We Slept: The Untold Story of Pearl Harbor* (New York: Viking Penguin, 1981), pp. 495–496.

2. Gordon W. Prange with Donald M. Goldstein and Katherine V. Dillon, *December 7 1941: The Day the Japanese Attacked Pearl Harbor* (New York: McGraw Hill, 1988), p. 98.

3. Walter Lord, *Day of Infamy* (New York: Bantam, 1958), p. 48; Prange, *December 7*, p. 99.

4. Prange, *December 7*, pp. 109–110.

Chapter 4. The Attack

1. Gordon W. Prange with Donald M. Goldstein and Katherine V. Dillon, *December 7 1941: The Day the Japanese Attacked Pearl Harbor* (New York: McGraw Hill, 1988), p. 114.

2. Prange, *December 7*, p. 164; Rear Admiral Edwin T. Layton with Captain Roger Pineau and John Costello, *And I Was There: Pearl Harbor and Midway—Breaking the Secrets* (New York: W. Morrow, 1985), p. 312.

3. Gordon W. Prange in collaboration with Donald M. Goldstein and Katherine V. Dillon, *At Dawn We Slept: The Untold Story of Pearl Harbor* (New York: Viking Penguin, 1981), pp. 527, 553; Robert E. Sherwood, *Roosevelt and Hopkins: An Intimate History* (New York: Harper, 1948), p. 431; Frank Freidel, *Franklin D. Roosevelt: A Rendezvous With Destiny* (Boston: Little Brown, 1990), p. 404.

4. Prange, *December 7*, p. 120.

5. Robert La Forte and Ronald Marcello, eds., *Remembering Pearl Harbor: Eyewitness Accounts by U.S. Military Men and Women* (Wilmington: SR Books, 1991), p. 29.

6. La Forte, *Remembering Pearl Harbor*, p. 30.

7. Prange, *December 7*, pp. 142–144.

8. Michael Slackman, *Target: Pearl Harbor* (Honolulu: University of Hawaii Press, 1990), pp. 120–121.

9. Prange, *At Dawn We Slept*, p. 507.

10. Donald Goldstein, Katherine V. Dillon, and J. Michael Wenger, *The Way It Was: Pearl Harbor— the Original Photographs* (Washington: Brassey's, 1991), p. 98.

11. Slackman, *Target*, pp. 165, 167.

12. Slackman, *Target,* pp. 109–110; Prange, *December 7,* pp. 148–149, 153; Doris Kearns Goodwin, *No Ordinary Time* (New York: Simon and Schuster, 1994), pp. 328–330.

13. Walter Lord, *Day of Infamy* (New York: Bantam, 1958), pp. 93, 185–187.

14. Stephen B. Young, "God, Please Get Us Out of This," *American Heritage* (April 1966), p. 110.

15. Slackman, *Target,* p. 105.

16. Prange, *December 7,* p. 193.

17. Ibid., p. 295.

18. Slackman, *Target,* pp. 132–133.

19. Thomas B. Allen, "Pearl Harbor: A Return to the Day of Infamy," *National Geographic* (December 1991), p. 66.

20. Slackman, *Target,* pp. 146–150.

21. Kathleen Warnes, "Nurses Under Fire: Healing and Heroism in the South Pacific," in Gunter Bischoff and Robert L. Dupont, eds., *The Pacific War Revisited* (Baton Rouge: Louisiana State University Press, 1997), p. 140.

22. Warnes, "Nurses Under Fire," pp. 139–142.

23. Slackman, *Target,* pp. 148–152; Stanley Weintraub, *Long Day's Journey into War* (New York: Plume, 1992), pp. 247–248.

24. Lord, *Day of Infamy,* p. 127.

25. Prange, *December 7,* pp. 192–193.

Chapter 5. A Devastating Loss

1. Alvin Coox, "The Pearl Harbor Raid Revisited," *Journal of American–East Asian Relations* (Fall 1994), pp. 221–223; Samuel Eliot Morison, *The Rising Sun in the Pacific* (Boston: Houghton Mifflin, 1958), p. 127.

2. David Smurthwaite, *The Pacific War Atlas, 1941–1945* (New York: Facts on File, 1995), p. 27; Gordon W. Prange with Donald M. Goldstein and Katherine V. Dillon, *God's Samurai: Lead Pilot at Pearl Harbor* (Washington: Brassey's, 1990), pp. 38–41.

3. Coox, "Pearl Harbor Raid," p. 223; Rear Admiral Edwin T. Layton, with Captain Roger Pineau and John Costello, *And I Was There: Pearl Harbor and Midway—Breaking the Secrets* (New York: W. Morrow, 1985), p. 322.

4. Michael Slackman, *Target: Pearl Harbor* (Honolulu: University of Hawaii Press, 1990), pp. 263–271.

5. Ibid, pp. 236–237.

6. Coox, "Pearl Harbor Raid," p. 225.

Chapter 6. The Aftermath

1. Author interview with Martha Branneman Gibbs, October 9, 1997.

2. Michael Slackman, *Target: Pearl Harbor* (Honolulu: University of Hawaii Press, 1990), p. 205; Walter Lord, *Day of Infamy* (New York: Bantam, 1958), p. 168.

3. Doris Kearns Goodwin, *No Ordinary Time* (New York: Simon and Schuster, 1994), p. 295.

4. Mark Jonathan Harris, Franklin D. Mitchell, Steven J. Schechter, *The Homefront: America During World War II* (New York: Putnam, 1984), p. 29.

5. Harris, *Homefront,* p. 85.

6. Ibid., pp. 27–28.

7. Michael H. Hunt, *Crises in U.S. Foreign Policy* (New Haven: Yale University Press, 1996), pp. 110–111; Samuel I. Rosenman, *Working With Roosevelt* (New York: Harper, 1952), p. 311.

8. Warren F. Kimball, *Forged in War: Roosevelt, Churchill, and the Second World War* (New York: W. Morrow, 1997), pp. 122, 131; Goodwin, *No Ordinary Time,* p. 290; Harris, *Homefront,* p. 141.

9. Goodwin, *No Ordinary Time,* pp. 313–314.

10. Harris, *Homefront,* p. 39.

11. John W. Dower, *War Without Mercy: Race and Power in the Pacific War* (New York: Pantheon, 1986), p. 80.

12. Dower, *War,* pp. 79, 82; John Morton Blum, *V Was for Victory: Politics and American Culture During World War II* (New York: Harcourt Brace Jovanovich, 1976), pp. 155–167.

Chapter 7. The War in the Pacific

1. Wayne S. Cole, *Roosevelt & the Isolationists* (Lincoln: University of Nebraska Press, 1983),

p. 508; H. P. Wilmott, *Empires in the Balance: Japanese and Allied Strategies to April 1942* (Annapolis: Naval Institute Press, 1982), pp. 141–142.

2. Mitsuo Fuchida and Masatake Okumiya, *Midway: The Battle that Doomed Japan* (Annapolis: Naval Institute Press, 1955), pp. 53–54.

3. Forrest C. Pogue, *George C. Marshall: Ordeal and Hope* (New York: Viking, 1966), p. 325.

4. Eric Bergerud, *Touched with Fire: The Land War in the South Pacific* (New York: Viking, 1996), pp. 311–312.

5. Bergerud, *Touched With Fire*, p. 38.

6. Ibid., pp. 299–302.

7. Ronald Spector, *Eagle Against the Sun: The American War with Japan* (New York: The Free Press, 1985), p. 294.

8. N. D. Kristof, "Japan Confronting Gruesome War Atrocity," *The New York Times*, March 17, 1995, p. 1; Mikiso Hane, *Peasants, Rebels, & Outcasts: The Underside of Modern Japan* (New York: Pantheon, 1982), p. 237.

9. Christopher Thorne, *The Issue of War: States, Societies and the Far Eastern Conflict of 1941–1945* (New York: Oxford University Press, 1985), p. 121.

10. Robert B. Edgerton, *Warriors of the Rising Sun: A History of the Japanese Military* (New York: Norton, 1997), p. 283; John W. Dower, *War*

Without Mercy: Race and Power in the Pacific War (New York: Pantheon, 1986), pp. 48–49.

11. James J. Weingartner, "Trophies of War: U.S. Troops and the Mutilation of Japanese War Dead, 1941–1945," *Pacific Historical Review* (February 1992), pp. 53–67.

12. J. Samuel Walker, *Prompt & Utter Destruction: Truman and the Use of Atomic Bombs Against Japan* (Chapel Hill: University of North Carolina Press, 1997), p. 1.

13. Roger Dingman, "Reflections on Pearl Harbor Anniversaries Past," *The Journal of American–East Asian Relations* (Fall 1994) p. 293; Arthur L. Kelly, *Battle Fire! Combat Stories from World War II* (Lexington: University of Kentucky Press, 1997), p. 14.

☆ **FURTHER READING** ☆

Black, Wallace, and Jean F. Blashfield. *Pearl Harbor!* Parsippany, N.J.: Silver Burdett Press, 1991.

Dunnahoo, Terry. *Pearl Harbor: America Enters the War.* New York: Franklin Watts, 1991.

Hopkinson, Deborah. *Pearl Harbor.* Parsippany, N.J.: Silver Burdett Press, 1991.

Nardo, Don. *World War II: The War in the Pacific.* San Diego: Lucent Books, 1991.

Rice, Earl. *The Attack on Pearl Harbor.* San Diego: Lucent Books, 1996.

_____. *The Battle of Midway: Battles of World War II.* San Diego: Lucent Books, 1996.

Stein, R. Conrad. *The USS Arizona.* Danbury, Conn.: Children's Press, 1992.

Sullivan, George. *The Day Pearl Harbor was Bombed.* New York: Scholastic, 1991.

Wills, Charles. *Pearl Harbor.* Parsippany, N.J.: Silver Burdett Press, 1991.

☆ INDEX ☆